A POETRY COLLECTION

KESS COSTALES

To my mother,

**You've always been
my guiding light**

CONTENT WARNING:
Depression, Anxiety, Suicidal thoughts,
Self-harm, Illness

TABLE OF CONTENTS

Author's note _________________ 5

Part 1: In the Dark___________ 7

Part 2: In the Light _________ 122

Acknowledgements________ 244

About the Author___________ 245

Author's note

I don't know exactly when I first started exhibiting signs of mental illness. I think my experience with social anxiety disorder started long before anyone could realize it. People have always called me shy and many have told me throughout my life that I would grow out of it as I grew more confident. It didn't seem to be true as I got more anxious in social situations as I got older.

And then, by my final years of high school, something more serious was happening that threatened not only my well-being, but my life. It became more evident very slowly. I described it to mental health professionals as something that progressed with time. Not so much sadness as much as feeling less and less interested in life and all the different parts of it. A lack of motivation, less inspiration, less eagerness to take on a new day. From infrequent moments to weekly ones, and then daily experiences of feeling these kinds of ways. And then it wasn't just every day, but all day. All the time.

By twelfth grade, my final year of high school, I was diagnosed with depression and anxiety. They go hand-in-hand a lot of the time, they said. Totally normal. Sometimes people get it without any triggers or traumas. Sometimes it's just what happens as the brain changes as we grow older.

I was seventeen when I made a suicide attempt. I considered it many more times after that, but following my attempt, I went through a lot of treatment. I spoke to psychiatrists and social workers and read every pamphlet available on depression and anxiety. While I was in the hospital, I met a psychiatrist who realized I didn't just have general anxiety. With some testing, it was determined that I also had social anxiety disorder, or social phobia. I think identifying that was the life-changing moment for me as we were able to figure out what I could work on to improve my mental health.

The problem is that these are chronic disorders for me. Periods of depression will come and go. My anxiety disorders will be easier sometimes, harder to manage at others. And so it's a constant process of trying to take care of myself and confronting the terrible thoughts that sometimes fill my mind.

Mental illness is not something to romanticize. It is not beautiful to suffer. It does not make me or anyone else more interesting. It is a facet of my life and manyothers.
And so, with this poetry collection, I want to share the thoughts and feelings of my experiences as someone with mental illnesses.

Part 1: In the Dark

COMORBIDITY

They are two wolves
And I am a lamb.
When they rip me apart,
They don't take turns.

ANXIETY

This one is a quiet killer,
The poison slipped into your tea
A little bit at a time.

Suddenly, my heart hurts.
The world spins.
Chaos reigns.

And I cannot
B r e a t h e

DEPRESSION

There have been days when it doesn't get a name.
When my tongue is too twisted to say what it is.

I reuse metaphors. I should have new similes.
But it will always be the bad place,
The dark place, that low, sunken place—
Where I feel like I am contained
Within a space without light.

And this is where I'll die.

SOCIAL PHOBIA

I used to be so joyful, so innocent.
Then I became steeped in fear.

It's the way they look at me,
That slight shift when they speak,
The angle of their body near me.

It's that gaping space of silence
And how I will fill this empty well
With everything that frightens me.

EYES

When did I stop looking up?

Holding someone's gaze feels like torture,
Hands wrapped around thorns,
Blood dripping down my wrists.

I cannot look at them
As if it is the barrel of a gun
Rather than a window.

Terror strikes like lightning
And I am powerless against it.
How do you fight something like that?

TOO MUCH

Maybe it's my fault for feeling this way.
Maybe I want too much, need too much.
Maybe it's too much to ask for anything.
Maybe I shouldn't know longing the way I do.
Maybe I should stop wondering if it's true
And just accept that I am too much for anyone
And maybe I should just try to shrink
And maybe then I won't have to think
That maybe I am too much for this world.

Too much emotion,
Too much trouble,
Too much of what I shouldn't be.

EMOTIONAL HANGOVER

Some days, I am better than okay.
I soar through the skies,
Weightless.

And then I come crashing
Down
Down
Down
D
o
w
n

DAILY CLIMB

Every day, I hike higher and higher,
Hoping to endure a little more
Than the day I endured before.

And every day, I trip over my own toes.
I tumble down the mountain,
Breaking my bones along the way.
There it goes, another day
I failed to conquer.

At the base of the mountain,
I am weeping and bleeding and wondering,
Will I ever have the strength to accomplish this climb?

NO LIGHT

Snuff out the flame,
Take away the warmth
And the guides along your path.

Close your eyes,
Hold your hands to your sides,
To discover if you already know the way.

Every step feels like creeping closer to the edge of a
cliff, where sharp rocks wait down below and yet the
image that burns into your eyelids isn't as scary as it is
alluring.

SURVIVAL

It may not seem like much
But every day is an exercise of survival.
I am weak-boned and weary,
Struggling to emerge from of this sanctuary
Made out of hours of sleep.
To go on, to keep going, to stay alive—
I have to wake and rise and fight.
I have to convince myself of things
that seem easy but aren't.

Imagine resistance to a simple glass of water,
Or curling your lip in disgust
At a slice of warm, toasted bread
Slathered in butter and honey.
My body doesn't crave any of that.
It doesn't want what it needs.
Instead, it wails in defeat.

It wants me to lay down and give up
As if I've been walking for days in a desert.
No end to the dunes, no hope in sight.
When I reach this point,
I have to teach myself
To get up,
To have a drink,
To take a bite,
To do enough

To survive a little longer.

The other option is
No survival.

THE WORST PART

Even though I was born in a snowstorm, I think I was meant for the sunlight. To have it kiss my skin the way it does in the depths of summer when you tilt your head back for the warmth and close your eyes in hopes of a breeze too. I grew up wearing the brightest colours and the biggest smiles with laughs so loud that the house would tremble. I think our home wanted to laugh with me.

Our homes were always small and our selection of food limited, but my mother kept our bellies full and kept our minds sharp. I learned that love is hugs and laughter and a hand holding yours when the nights feel long. When my mother would sit in bed with a book, I'd grab one to sit with her too, though I'd read it upside down and she'd just smile and set it right. With my sister, I followed her everywhere and tried to do anything she wanted just to get as much time with her as I could.

I grew up wearing dresses and bows and loving pink and purple and yellow. I grew up trying to make my family laugh, dancing and wiggling and trying to say the sweetest things because I knew they liked that. We watched Disney movies on repeat, rewind and start over, and fall in love with the stories and songs again and again. I sang for my family and for my friends, holding the microphone for karaoke like it was the only thing I knew.

We played games in which we became princesses or like pirates. We went to parks and museums, to restaurants and play places, on trails up mountains or over to waterfalls, and all sorts of adventures. There was so much love and adventure that you could not argue that I had a good childhood.

So, maybe the worst part is that I still ended up sad. Grieving for something I couldn't see or name or say what it was. All I knew was that slowly, slowly, slowly… the sun wasn't so bright and the rain was rather gloomy and the warm days and cold days were no different from each other. All the days felt wrong and awkward and unappealing. All the nights felt like a curse with no cure, a plague set on me by a witch who didn't exist and, as such, they couldn't offer me a way to find relief.

I was sweet by nature and we nurtured that even more.

And that didn't change anything. I don't think the past was set and I don't think anything or anyone was at fault for what I felt. It was what it was and maybe the worst part could be that I was afraid my mother blamed herself.

It wasn't her. Or anyone. Or anything. It was what it was.

And so, maybe the worst part is that no matter how much I was loved and how happy I was as a little girl, that didn't change anything.

HIDE

Battle after battle, never winning.
Always losing, always failing,
Always being weaker and smaller and fragile.

Tear-stained and scarred,
Red-eyed and grimacing,
Bone-thin and weary.

I cannot go on like this.
I cannot look at myself like this.

The sight makes me shatter mirrors.
I'll build a prison cell of the shards
And shackle myself with the rest.

TELL ME WHERE

I cannot see the good in me.
The mirror only knows to be mocking.
My mind swirls with disdain for life, for myself.

So where is the good in me?
Can you see any worthiness?
I am ignorant of it,
I doubt its existence.

Tell me where it exists
And tell me it's true.

ALL BAD

When I was little, I developed a habit:
hiding when I felt I had done wrong.
They do that on TV,
the parents sending the children aside.

Think of what you did.
Take a time out.
Sit in the corner.
Spend some time alone.

I burrowed under the stairs
Or hid inside the closet.
No lights, all dark,
Sitting in silence.

I thought I deserved that.
I thought I should be punished
For anything that was bad.

And if I did one bad thing,
I was all bad. All of me and everything I could do.
All bad and no good and therefore
I should go away. I should disappear.
It would be better for everyone if I did.

(How does a little girl decide that?)

It seemed simpler back in the day,
When I could paint my world
In swaths of black and white,
Not a chance for one speck of grey.

WRONG

I don't know anything
From how to speak
To how to breathe just right.

I can't do anything
In a way that makes you smile
So I must be wrong.

But what exactly?
Maybe all of me
From the way my eyes crinkle
To the slice of my smile
And the way my body folds
When I am told
By that little voice in my mind
That I cannot do any good.

It's easy to say that I could
Be the child the stood
With her head high
And her heart sure
That she could always get by
So long as she believed
That she could do
Whatever she wanted to.

Instead I worried

That it was never enough
No matter what I tried,
And so I just wanted to hide
To ensure that no one could see
How wrong I could be.

BARBED WIRES

I've become an expert at hiding the danger,
Of coating barbed wires in thick honey.
I've made masks of painted porcelain,
Patching up the cracks on the daily.
I've started wrapping the knife in silk,
Pretending to tuck it away
When it's sinking into my skin.

HEARTACHE

I've become used to the feeling
Of strings snapping suddenly.
Cable wires coming apart,
And the only way to go
is crashing down with
wires burrowing into my skin,
then into my chest, into my heart,
into the place where it hurts the most.

Maybe it's a shovel,
Carving out the thing
That aches and aches.

I'm familiar with the endless agonies
But that echo, too, like my chest is empty.
It's something sharp and hollow
And I have to wonder what's happening
To my heart,
to me.

SHUT DOWN

There are days when all I want is to be numb,
To lock the doors and set the bolts in place.
A whisper creeps against my ear,
Saying *no one would want the mess inside*.
It would be easier to shut down,
Run and hide and stop struggling
To stay alive.

SOME HEARTS

Some hearts are cold and closed-off.
Some are so hot, they're overheating.
Some days I think I'm the first,
But then maybe I'm the other.

My heart is so overwhelmed
That it burns and cracks and comes apart.
It's fire and ice and it hurts all the same.

DO NOT DO IT

Don't hold onto someone
who already let you go.

Don't look where they once stood
when they already walked away.

Don't keep in them in your heart
if they already closed theirs.

Don't dream of them
especially if they don't dream of you.

STOP LOOKING

You peeked at my pictures, my story—
Only for the shortest of seconds.

You'll close your eyes to stop yourself,
Your mind, from wondering about me.
And yet I'll keep wondering about you.

THE SERPENT

Somewhere along the way
Questions come to mind.

Would they miss me?
Would they care?
Would they even notice?

And this serpentine thing whispers into my ear
With a hiss and a flick of its forked tongue,
No, not you. Of course not.

Such poisonous words to sound true.

BIRDS PT. 1

If I was a bird,
I'd be wearing broken wings.
No songs emerging from me,
No love or joy to sing.

PRAYER

I stopped looking for angels in the sky.
Don't press my palms together in prayer.
When I whisper under my breath,
I no longer call out to my god.

If he's out there, if he's real,
Then why won't he hear me?

That is all I can ask of him now.

HALO

Good girls wear a halo over their head.
They pull their glossy lips into smiles,
Dab sweet perfumes on their wrists.

Good girls wrap ribbons over the scars
Like bracelets made of white satin,
Bloodstained on the other side.

My halo is only fluorescence.
My ribbons are my reminders
That as good as I can be
It is never good enough.

WICKED

I am a wicked creature
With a soul destined for hell.
There are terrible things I feel
And worse things I could never tell.

If I was good,
Would my mind
Be so unkind?

BAD PERSON

I am not a good person
When I cannot do the right thing
And I see the way words sting
As I fail to make up my mind.
How could that be kind
To hurt people all the time
No matter how hard I try
Or how good I aim to be.
It doesn't come easily.

And so I cannot be good,
Always failing to do what I should
To make others happy.

I must be bad then,
Making others sadden.
It makes me hate myself
For something I cannot help
Because trying to avoid the hurt
Never seems to work.

Am I a bad person?
I want to be gentle and sweet
Yet only manage to worsen
The lives of people I meet.

REAL OR NOT

Are these thoughts in my head
Things to fear or things to ignore?
If I go to where I am led,
Could I accept what's in store
For me in this place
Where I'm in a space
Filled with spite and cruelty?

It's hard to say that I can
Look at my loved ones today
And believe that they truly care
About the things I do and say.
My mind tells me wicked things
And I can't tell them apart
The things valid in my heart
From the things untrue
About all that I do
And who I really am.

I hate not knowing
And I'm afraid of it showing
That I'm lost in this battle
Of wondering what's real
And what's not.

S.O.S.

Save our souls, let me live in peace or let me be free.
Save my soul, tell me there's somewhere to go.
I want to hope there's a better place to be
Because here, all I know is hurting.

FRAYED ROPE

Hope is barely more than a frayed rope.
I hold onto the end of it, wondering,
Do I climb up or do I let go?
It feels like it will come apart anyway.

WISHING

There are a hundred coins in the water now, sunk to the bottom and sitting untouched. I think each one has a bit of my heart in it, and I've been tossing it away every time I've tried to make a wish. All I am is emptying my wallet. I am wasting metal on a moment. I am throwing my hope into the air and waiting to see where it will land.

And it always falls into the dark water.
What does that say about me?

Maybe I should be plucking petals from daisies these days, wondering what the outcome will be. I switch between my questions, guilty about the first one that always comes to mind. The one that isn't something I can say aloud. You'll gasp and call me morbid. You'll tell me I shouldn't wish for such a thing. That big wish in my heart that shouldn't be something I want ever, at all. I feel like I'm wishing for nothing instead, wasting my wishes on things that make me sad. Spending wishes like my heart is a jukebox and the song I keep choosing is one that makes me cry.

I rip at the petals now like it's a scab that I'm determined to turn into a scar. When I set my fingers on the softness, I turn violent, angry. This isn't working, this trying to make a game out of my emotions. I find myself tearing through flowers like I am a blade. I cut them at the stem, snap them like twigs. I stare at them, searching for imperfections. Does it count if the petals are already a bit ripped? Do the small ones matter less than the others?

I want to stand at the wishing well without wondering if I should jump inside. I want to pick up a flower to marvel at it, not to think if tearing it apart might make me feel better. I want to make a wish and feel hopeful. I don't want to hurt.

DON'T

Don't reach out.
Don't hold on.
Don't give away
Pieces of your heart.

Don't break.
Don't shatter.
Don't pick up the shards
When you do.

BREAKABLE

I am not glass.
I am not porcelain.
I am still somehow
This breakable thing.

THE COST

I can't afford to make myself vulnerable.
I am already all loose threads.
If you pull at me, I'll unravel.

THE DOOR

After I've been hurt,
I try to close the door I once opened.
Sometimes I will peek at the other side,
Opening the door enough for an eye.

You had me in the doorway,
Standing with no distance between us.
Now I have to use this barrier
To shield myself
From something that might never be mine.

SENSITIVITY

Like the sweetest apple,
I am easily bruised.
Be gentle with me.
When you hold me,
Be careful.
You could crush me
In the palm of your hand.

APOLOGIES

There are apologies hanging at the back of my throat
Like they're climbing to the peak of mountain,
Almost about to fail to grab onto the next ledge.
Something in my head tells me that despite all the love
And all the joy and all the good I can have
This is a temporary high, destined to head south.

I feel like I should always say sorry
And it's always the same story
That I think there's nothing I do right
As much as I try with all my might
To make my loved ones happy.

SORRY AGAIN

What I'd like is to forget what I've done,
To pretend I didn't hurt anyone.
All I have are my tears and my apologies.

I am sorry I am sorry I am sorry

And I hope you won't hate me
As much as I hate myself.

(No one could ever match that)

HOW IT SOUNDS

Doesn't it sound sad to hear me say things like that?
The problem is that it's all true.
I hate myself. I hurt myself. I hate the way things are.
And it isn't because of you
or someone or something that happened.

That makes it sound silly, or maybe asinine.
It sounds like a problem I've built up in my mind,
Instead of a real thing
That is utterly terrifying.

I have nightmares about this:
Trying to say what it is,
And how it only sounds
Like a bad story.

ARGUMENTS

We are locked in a screaming match,
My mind and I.

We don't know what we want or need—
To live or to die or something in between.

We say yes, we say no,
We cannot agree
We cannot see
Eye to eye.

We cannot find peace.
We scream, swords crossed.
Ready to strike.
Ready to surrender.

We are trapped in a cycle of arguments,
In a war neither of us can win.

THE EXPLANATION

How do you say how much it hurts?
Like the jaws of life
Pulling my ribcage apart.
Or sticking screws beneath my feet
And trying to stand on them.

Sometimes it's not as much as that.
It could be a hollowness
Like carving a pumpkin clean.

That isn't pretty. That isn't a good explanation.

What I feel doesn't make sense.
How do I explain the lack of wounds?
How do I show you where it hurts?

It is everywhere, all the time.

THIS CREATION

Everything I feel makes me into a monster,
The kind that turns vicious when afraid.

THE TRANSFORMATION

I think I transform into a beast in the night. Dark thoughts come forward. I become something cruel, something unkind, something bitter and afraid. I am feral from the fear. I am nothing but a beast, unleashed, attacking anyone who comes near me because I cannot believe that anyone would not wish me harm.

Be weary. Watch my every move. Let me show you how terrible this beast can be.

I transform into this violent thing, incapable of trust. Aimless, angry, uncertain. Snap my jaws over an unsuspecting throat. Sink my fangs into someone soft and vulnerable. Dig my nails under their skin as I bite harder and harder until they hurt as much as I do.

While they are bleeding, I look unaffected. On the outside, I am intact, untouched. Inside, I am nothing but guts and gore. I am rotting, long since ruined.

WILD ANIMALS

There is a wolf nipping at my heels,
Chasing me into the woods
Far beyond the safety of my home.

There is a bear with its paws on my chest
And its weight is heavy on top of me.
I think my bones might already be broken.

There is a monster beneath my bed
That crawls out when the lights are off
And exhales its rancid breath in my face.

There is also something bigger—
Something stronger and more frightening
Figuring out the way to make me shake,
Making me feel small and unsafe and so close
To shattering.

MY OWN WICKEDNESS

Sometimes the beast isn't inside of me; it is me. Sometimes I am the thing that you should fear when my mood is sour and my heart is aching. That is when I am at my worst, when I am loud and I have my voice, when I bare my teeth and reach my arms out to strike. I am small and overemotional. When I feel, it is all too much, and it comes out of me in a relentless rush that can be violent and volatile.

I seek to be kind and to know nothing of kindness, but I know cruelty. Not because I sat at the knee of monsters and sought to take up their trade. Not because I searched for someone to show me how to use the weapons I've been born to wield: these dark eyes and twisted tongue, these thin hands with long nails that claw at the air when I am angry, this heart that gets wound up like a spring that will unleash a pouncing beast.

When I am in the dark place, I am the creature of horror stories. I emerge from the pit, grasp the ankles of those who pass me, and yank them into this abyss. Let them know the darkness too. Let them feel the terror. If I should suffer, so should they, and then we will all know how much it hurts. How awful it all is. How unfair it is that they cannot empathize deeply with what I endure on the daily.

When I become this wicked thing, I am not immediately aware of it. The words slip off my tongue like air exhaled on instinct. It feels natural, terrible as it is. My fears ricochet off me and everything around me, including the bodies of those who come close in hopes of aiding me. I am the whirlpool in a pitch-black ocean, a storm swirling above me. Everyone in my vicinity is sucked in and spun around and around in this violent cycle.

They try to save me from the monster, not realizing that it's been there all along. That it is me, rather than the thing trapping me. I am not the innocent princess in the tower, locked away by some witch. I was the one to snap the chains around my own ankles and wrists, the one to build my prison cell in solitary confinement of my own choosing, and the one who screams when they notice the shackles. I am the thing that lashes out when you try to offer comfort. I am hurting and I do not know how to manage it. I am hurting and I think it's trying to crawl out of me like a parasite, like this is a viral disease that is bound to infect others. And so, when I am feeling kind and I realize what damage I can cause, it is better to be alone. To suffer by myself. To keep others away and unaware of what is happening.

Sometimes there is no monster with me. Sometimes it is my own wickedness. Sometimes it's not something inside of me, it is who I have become.

That is, at least, how it feels.

KIDNAPPED

You want to be okay
But you don't know how.

It's a messy knot and your fingers can't seem to get
under the loops. Your hands won't stop shaking from the
cold. There are tears in your eyes and a scream lodged in
your throat. You are blindfolded and gagged. Your wrists
are tied together.

You want to be okay
But you have to wonder—
Is this how a hostage feels?

I am kidnapped by this tight, cold feeling.
I am hurting yet I cannot find the wound.
I want to be okay but I don't know how.

ONE LONG NIGHT

I can't remember the last sunrise
When I'm staring up at the night sky.

Does the darkness ever end?
It feels so much worse when there isn't a star in sight.

SUNSET PT. 1

When the day comes to an end
And the sun dips low in the sky,
Panic seizes me.

The night is coming,
The darkness too.
The shadows that call out,
Reach out, drag me into them.

When the sun starts to set,
I rediscover fear.

HOW TO BREATHE

The technique evades me,
A ghost I don't believe in,
Slipping away, unnoticed.
I am haunted by the memory
Of moments when I knew how to do this:
Just breathe.

All I know is this brick
That sits on my chest
And the duct tape
Over my mouth and nose.

And this feeling,
This knowledge
That I may die
That I *will* die
That I should die
If I cannot figure this out.

THAT FIRST BREATH

Open your eyes.
Greet the new day.

Take a breath. It hurts.
It's a knife down your throat.

You have to wonder
If your lungs are burning or bleeding,
And why your heart's always speeding.
There's chaos in my head
That comes to me while I'm still in bed
And exhausts me before I can rise.

There has to be more than this.
It feels like there is.
It isn't fair to feel this way
Every fucking day.

ONE CUT

I learned how to hide the self-hate.
One cut was all I needed.
Slice with a thin razor.
Let it bleed.
Let it heal
Slightly.

Then rip it open
And hide it under a ribbon.

LONELY

Feeling the need to be with someone
If it's just sitting side by side
Or holding hands like chain links
So that for a moment I don't have to think.
Wanting this makes me feel crazy,
Craving something so small and easy,
And it feels too great of a task
To even ask.

But wanting that closeness
And being afraid once it's mine,
Feels like staring into the sun.
It's warm but dangerous
To wonder what will become of us
If I shared what's on my mind.

It isn't joyful.
It's awful.
But maybe if someone's here,
If someone just stays near,
This fight won't be so lonely
When I have someone beside me.

FINDING LOVE

What scares me about love is not that I won't find it. I'm certain I will fall in love a hundred times in a hundred different ways, from the sound of rain against the windows to the warm smile you share when I tell you about how beautiful I think you are. That's not the frightening part because I know love will come to me in some shape or from.

Do you know anything about how love can feel? It's not just a warm embrace or a kiss on the forehead when you're drifting off to sleep and it's impossible to say if this is a dream or simply a perfect night. It's more than the delicate purring of a small kitten curled up on your chest after hours of it shivering and shaking in fear of its new home with strange smells, strange sounds, and stranger people. One might say that it can be like that, or both, or something completely different.

Sometimes I think that love is the way he looks at me, his chin in his hands and a smile he cannot stop making at the sight of me and the sound of my voice. But that could be a moment, captured just like that, and never once coming back to share a kiss. That could be love, or infatuation. It could be entirely one-sided, with my imagination building it up as something bigger than it is. Just looking at me, playing make-believe that I could have love with someone who can look at me like I'm the long-awaited sunshine after a series of grey storms.

Maybe he won't fall in love with me even if I fall for him. Maybe I'll end up chasing love like it's a butterfly and my heart is a torn net. I'm not scared about finding love because I know it's everywhere and all around me and somewhere within reach. Finding it isn't the problem. I fall in love all the time. I even fall in love with my friends in the least romantic yet whimsical way, adoring them for all the beautiful things they are—gentle and good or harsh and honest. I love them as a sister, as a friend, as someone who would fight to the death for them.

But finding love isn't the problem. I will find love. I will see it and crave it and wish upon stars to have it become mine. Maybe it won't be mine and that's a little terrifying, too. There's a chance I'll see it and hope for it and the rocket launch of my heart into the atmosphere of their existence will crash and burn and I will be picking at the pieces, trying to find where I went wrong in the rubble.

That's not what scares me about love, even if I am worried that it won't be mine.

No, what I'm afraid of most is that no one will love me as much as I learned to love myself.

And then I'll be alone.

I DON'T LIKE THIS

I do not like being on my knees.
I do not like to beg or plea.
I do not like the sad way you look at me.

WHO WOULD

There is a question constantly on my mind:
Who would want this?
This whirlwind of worrying, this broken heart,
This downward spiral of self-doubt?

Who would want this?
Sad eyes, downturned lips,
Half-hearted when I kiss.

Who would want this?
Lesser like this, smaller and scared.
I am not who I wish I was so who would want me?

I think I'm fated to be lonely.

WHO TO BE

I know what I should be doing:
Smiling wider, bowing my head,
Speaking softly, going where I'm led,
Using the twinge of my family's accent
To be less of product of where I'm kept
Though more than an ocean divides me
In this diverse city and the one I want to see.

This culture of ours wants me this way:
Grateful and docile and aware of my luxuries,
Proud but not haughty, bearing my family's worries
That coming here was a risk, a sacrifice
To do and be more than what would suffice.

They struggled. They fought. They survived
In a world of dreams but still strange
And maybe we would dream of the islands
Painted in jeweled tones of blue and green
Instead of cities of smoky grey and brown.

I should be fighting. Surviving. Dreaming.
I am closed-lipped and silently screaming.
I am soft bones and sensitive skin
And a bruised heart stretched thin.
I am weaker than I should be.
Too weak to stand comfortably.

I sway. I falter. I break.
I am not who I should be,
Built by those stronger than me.

I am failing,
Falling, not flying.
Struggling to just be.

FEELING

How silly it is
To dream about sleeping
But allow me to be romantic
About being my most vulnerable with you.
Unconscious, unaware of the world,
Yet certain that I am safe in your bed.

This terrible,
As agonizing as ripping apart my own skin.
To feel is to hurt and that's everything about us.
Hurting not because you are cruel or I am weak
But because I feel so much
About you and me and us.

I drown in emotion,
Head submerged and lungs bursting
Throat burning from lack of air.
Sometimes it is romantic,
Others it is simply sad.

I am almost always
Drowning in blue,
Wishing I was with you,

Instead of sinking
Down into the dark
again.

NOT OKAY

I am here
And you're over there
And what that means is
Everything
is not okay.

THE WELL

I catch myself at a wishing well
Praying for someone to save me.

And then I dive inside.

No one will look for me.

I will always remain there,
Buried under wishes
Half of which are mine
And none that ever came true.

A ROSE

One day
Someone will find me worthy.
They will fight for me on the field
All while holding my hand.

They'll bring me a flower
Red roses, red like painted lips,
Seeking a kiss in exchange.

But who looks at me and thinks like that?
I've let myself wander through an imaginary world.

There is no rose,
No person waiting to offer it.
There is only me,
Pressing my thumb into thorns.

FAR FROM

I am far from perfect.
There will always be
An echoing ache in me.

TOO PERFECT

You are this beautiful thing
Crafted out of marble by expert hands
And yet I cannot breathe life into you.

APART

We are statues, trapped in this position,
Where I am reaching and you are running.

RELUCTANCE

When I am with you,
I recognize how greedy I am.
How much I want to keep you
Like another bauble in my jewelry case.
How much I languish in your affection,
Lapping up your words, your praises.

How wicked of me to keep you,
To draw out the days and the inevitable:
I will hurt you and no matter what you say,
Part of you will resent me
And my reluctance to let you go.

But imagine me like one of Barrie's fairies,
Needing applause and applause to live.
I am not kind or gentle like you say,
I am not good-hearted or sugar sweet.
I am all sin and I have seduced you
With promises I could not keep.

This is awful of me,
This reluctance to end this thing.
This realization that I cannot continue trying
To force myself to feel what you deserve.

I do love you
But not how I should.

ROTTEN

Have you ever met a girl like me?
One covered in lace and lilac,
Pearls and pink, satin and sugar.
It's a costume, you see.
All that I adorn is ornament.

I may look nice,
But I am rotten inside.

FRAMES

When something is beautiful
And you want everything to see,
You place it in a gold case.

You line the sides of it with metal,
Stick it on the wall for display.

When you hate yourself in every way,
You lock yourself in a cage
Hidden in a dark, dark room
Where you will be unseen and then
Forgotten.

ADMISSION FEE

To see all the art, you pay a fee.
For me, there is no charge.
I am not worth even a penny.
No one comes to look at me and love me.

SHIVERS

It's cold, I'd say. *I'm freezing.*
My body keeps shaking, wracked by violent shivers
Like I'm a sapling struggling to stay upright
Against the tornado spinning toward me.

QUESTIONNAIRE

Do you like me?
Do you think I'm sweet?
Do you want to be friends?
Will you stay when all upends?

Do you find me exhausting?
Do you think everything's okay?
Do you wish you were somewhere else?
Do you wish I was someone else?

Do you see how afraid I am of what you think of me?
Do you see my racing thoughts like lights on the
highway?
Do you see my shaking hands and unsteady breaths?
Do you see how hard I'm trying to stay standing?

Do you see me slowly falling?
Do you know that I'm on the edge?
Do you think I should stay?

GROWING

I am still growing;
I don't know what I'll become.

I am still learning
Something useful, something scary.

I do not know how to live
Or if I want to at all.

WILTED

The problem with growing
Is that you're not always at your best.
Plants grow new blooms
Again and again
As the old ones wilt and die.

Right now, I am not blooming.
Wilted is what I am now
And how I've been for too long.

I want to be brighter, beautiful.
I want to be a myriad of colour.

But I am grey
And sad
And wilted
And almost dead.

EXOTIC FLOWERS

You called me exotic.
I wanted to be more.

Why did it have to be that word?

Let me be your everything
Or your world
Or the most amazing thing you've ever seen.

Exotic
Is one word
I don't want.

IMPERFECTIONS

Flowers are one of the most beautiful things
But even they are never perfect.

So why am I supposed to be?
Why do I demand perfection from myself?

TOO MUCH

Every now and then
I think I've come a long way.

Until someone reminds me
I'm not as lovely as they thought I could be.
There is too much terror, too much hurt,
Too many tear stains on my shirt.

I am crying and I am in pain
And it's too much for someone again.

GRASS

Lay in the wet green
Early in the morning
And tell me of the discomfort.

It's cold and seeps through your clothes
Onto your skin, then under it.
You shiver and want to escape the sensations.

Imagine feeling that way
Whenever you wake up,
Yet you're still laying in bed.

OCEAN WATER

Falling onto your hands in the ocean at night
When you can't tell apart the sky from the water
And you don't know what might sneak up on you

Is almost like peering into the dark of my mind
And not sure which monsters will snap at me.

I am terrified but I can't stop myself
From the descent.

SINKING

Someone has strapped a bag of rocks over my shoulders
and I am
Sinking
Sinking
Sinking
Somewhere dark blue
Somewhere disturbingly cold.

I am under crashing waves,
Still in this world,
But unable to breathe.

GOLD

All my life I have felt dull,
Like there isn't enough shine to me
And I couldn't ever really glow.

I always wanted to be golden.
But at best, I am only beige.

GRAVEYARD

I despised the hospital.
White sheets, white walls, locked windows and doors.
The rancid smell of coarse bed sheets and bleach,
With all the disinfectant hanging in the air.
Close your eyes and you'll hear the sway
Of plastic tubes and metal chains
That plunge medicine into your veins
And calculate every tired heartbeat.

The hospital is one step closer to a graveyard
And when the doctors and nurses hover over me,
I almost wish I was already there.

HEADSTONE

What will they say about me
Right above my grave?

Dear beloved daughter, dearly depressed.

The stone at the head of where I rest
Is a tablet of little details:
My birth, my death, who still loved me.

My name engraved,
And all that's left of me.

EMBALMING ME

In my head,
I hold morbid thoughts.
When I push lotion over my arms,
All I can think is
About a dead body.

Mine,
Embalmed,
Prepared for a funeral.

People shouldn't dream about this.

DECAY

Some days, the bed is a grave
And it is deeper than it seems.
The body cannot move.
There is no way out.
All you can see is the space above
And know that you will remain below.

When you try to breathe,
All you get is dirt in lungs
And the taste of your death.
It's rot in your mouth,
Your own slow decay.

LIVING DEAD

Other days, you are alive
But barely.

When you walk, it is a slow, unsteady pace
Of swaying side to side on weak legs
And feet that ache under your unwilling body.

Eyes strain to stay open,
Arms outstretched in hopes of grasping something
Like pulling yourself forward
before you fall to the ground
As if your bones want to sink into the earth.

You walk among the living,
Though your heart is still beating,
You don't feel eager to be alive.

DEVIL'S ADVOCATE

You don't need to play the role for me,
Of the devil in my ear.
He's already in my head,
Saying things I don't need to hear.

No, don't play the devil's advocate.
His voice is here in my mind,
Echoing and echoing all the damn time.

THE VAST UNIVERSE

When the skies are clear
And the stars fill in the darkness,
I am struck with wonder and
Terror.

What am I compared to what's out there?
Small and insignificant, nothing at all,
Not even a bright speck in the sky.

So in the dark of the night
I have my darkest thought:
If I was gone, it wouldn't make a difference
In the context of the vast, unending universe.

AND SO ON

So so so sad
So so so sorry
So so so sick

Of existing

NO PRETENDING

At some point,
It stopped mattering.

The play of being okay
Concluded without a curtain closing,
As if the main actress just turned
And exited the stage.

I did not care.
I could no longer pretend.

I was miserable, bruised by feeling,
Black and blue with grief
Though no one had died.

And yet, though I knew something was wrong,
I failed to see what I'd transformed into.

THE LOW POINTS

You cannot count them like numbers on a scoreboard
Like dots on dice, or the fingers of your hand.
You cannot tell time as clearly as you normally could,
Like the arms on the clock bend in odd sorts of ways.

All you know is that you've sunk,
Down down down
Into this place
Of darkness, no sky in sight,
And you cannot climb out.

HALFWAY THERE

Almost dead,
Could have died,
Should have.

It's a terrible thought
That infects my mind.

When my lungs filled with liquid
And my body was too weak to fight,
I thought I was halfway to the afterlife.

ALL IN

I talk about this too much—
The knife too dull
To do what I wanted,
The screaming
because I wasn't
strong enough.

TWO TOO BROKEN

It was supposed to be the step up to greatness,
You and me all on our own, taking on everything.
Years led us to that place to stand on two feet,
Hand in hand and confident like we had everything.

We broke each other's hearts though.
In trying to be happy and being together,
It seemed we couldn't have both.
And that hurt you, hurt me, hurt us,
Hurt so much of our being that we just
Couldn't be anymore.

To heal meant to go separate ways
And I hated saying goodbye.
It was a necessary evil to fight,
Acting like the heroes of our own stories.

It was easier to cover our eyes,
Pretend we couldn't see the blatant fact
That we could not keep us intact
When we both had broken pieces
With edges that didn't align.

TO BABY ME

You will learn to hate
To fear and resent and regret.
And when things go wrong,
You will blame yourself.
You will punish yourself.

I want to warn you
In hopes that you'll learn to battle
When all I could do was cry.

THE INNOCENCE

You didn't always know about this dark place.
You didn't know you would walk through that labyrinth.
Growing up meant giving up some of that innocence
That all children have when they are loved and protected.

You didn't always know long stretches of cloudy days
Or that some days you wouldn't find the sun anywhere.
You had the innocence of a little girl
living in daydreams,
Where the sky was pink and the clouds were candy.

You didn't always feel so low, so broken and unsure,
As if there were missing parts you'd never find.
You didn't always think you were assembled wrong,
That you were not missing anything,
you just weren't right.

VANITY

Your vanity will stop you
From carving the razor deep.
Your vanity will keep you
From scarring, from reminders.

And while the cuts wouldn't remain,
It will take a very long time to heal.

Later, you'll find yourself in that place again,
Trying to remember the path to feeling better,
Before realizing you have to pave a new way.

There are no physical markings
Of all the bad things you felt.
But they will be there.

WRECKAGE

If you look right here,
You'll find the wreckage in me,
Shards under the skin.

THE BREAKING

When you have a romantic heart,
You let yourself fall so many times,
It's like you've thrown your body down a staircase.

Every step is another failed attempt to fall in love.
I think this is the way I like to hurt myself.
To see that I want this love and it won't be mine.
That maybe I cannot ever have the love I want.

And what is life without love?

In these moments, I am forgetting that love
Exists in all sorts of ways.

MAYBE NOT

We try, we cry, we go on and on.
A new connection, another lost.
Maybe everything will work.
Maybe nothing will.

Maybe I'll relearn happiness
Like it's instinct.

Maybe not.

BITTER HEART

Here is where I will lay down the lines about the bites my heart has had to make in recent days. The sun stays in the sky longer as we inch closer to summer, but the lonely state of my heart sets me in the shadows, sulking, sad. I am pouting as I look out the window, watching grey skies and quiet streets and wondering how long I'll be alone. My heart is angry and afraid, and I fear it will become a feral thing in an uncertain world. I am so used to affection that I do not know how to breathe without it, and I think that is dangerous. I think I am placing needles into the sole of my foot, trying to make something I can stand upon. I keep putting my weight onto those feet and screech at the pain of settling my weight on each point. It is a shark's mouth against my skin, teeth sinking into me.

Here is where I weep and lay my head, hiding beneath the blankets that no longer feel like a fort to protect me from invaders and conquerors. I think I am afraid and I forgot my armour somewhere on the path to this sad sanctuary that reeks of sweat and stale air. The windows have been open, but I've scarcely stepped outside. It is a new, unfamiliar world out there and I don't have a map to help me navigate it. I don't know if I'll recognize the streets or if I'll be terrified of the faces half-hidden by masks so that we can breathe without fear. I think, however, that I will always be afraid, and my body will cling to that feeling like a lifejacket when it's really the rocks tied to my limbs.

Here is where my heart turns bitter. I don't think I can fall in love in a world like this. I don't know if I could ever become someone's favourite person when we are all cynics or stressed or a little bit of both. How am I supposed to be hopeful when the days blur together and the world is changing too quickly to count the warped shapes and try to understand the new language we're weaving? We live in intensity and insanity and I think my heart should turn to stone to survive.

But no. Here, I feel too much. I reach and jump and crash again and again and I look at the faces, at the names, at all the messages we could exchange and think about how none of this will work.

And none of this will matter.

My bitter heart has decided in this loneliness that this is all I can have.

THOUSANDS

When your heart breaks
A thousand times
And you have to rebuild
A thousand times
You'll have
A thousand
Different
Versions
Of
The
Same
Aching.

PAY ATTENTION

If your heart isn't hurting
And your rage isn't burning,
You aren't paying attention.

If you don't understand
How this agony emerges,
You need to seek education.

People die every day
But they shouldn't perish
Over things we could conquer
Together.

HOPEFUL

The girl I used to be
Saw the world in bright colours.
Endless options, a rainbow stretching across the sky.

The one I became
Can't remember the warmth in the light.
Can't remember what it feels like to hope,
To believe that there are better days.

When I'm hopeful, I'll know I'm better.
Today, I'm still at my worst.

ALL I HAVE

Let me first apologize,
I don't have much to offer.
My hands are empty,
My smiles are sad,
My heart feels hollow.

All I have is this life
I've tried to cut down with a knife
And a head full of words
Either wicked or wistful.

All I have are these words,
This rambling like I'm running out of time.

What if I am?
What are these words worth?

THE CLIFF

Think of the edge of a cliff.
If you're standing at the edge,
You might not need anyone
Because you can always step away.

But if you're hanging from the edge,
It may be good to have someone there
To help you find your footing.

SOMETHING SHINING

There is a little bit of light,
Like a lit match in the night,
Like someone has found me
Underneath all the rubble.

There is something shining here,
Like someone is drawing near,
Filling the dark with a flashlight.

I think I have forgotten how bright
Things could be in contrast to
This long, dark night.

The sun is rising.
Maybe so am I.

LIGHT IN THE TUNNEL

When there finally seems to be a light,
You know you're reaching the end.

Or at least a way out of this abyss.

Part 2: In the Light

FIRST LOOK

Think about the sunlight,
Filtering through the window:
How its warmth spreads across your bed
And fans gentle heat over your cheeks.
When you open your eyes,
It's all you see.

This great, golden thing.

MELLOWED

I remember the morning
When the pills started working.
We sat on the bed and I was silent.
I was calmer, instead of crying.

Mellow, I said. *Chilled out.*
When was the last time I felt that?
All that noise was static.
And it suddenly vanished.

GASPING

There is nothing like the first breath
After you've been rolling in the undertow,
Tumbling under crashing waves
In a dark ocean with a storm overhead.
I thought I was almost dead.
Then my feet found the ground,
And I could finally gasp for air.

REMEMBER THIS

You have done what seemed impossible.
You have survived the fight inside you.
You built up your strength and stamina
So that when you find yourself fighting again,
You'll know how to defeat your foe.

HOW LIGHT BURNS

Coming out of that deadly space
Feels a lot like the sunlight
Against your eyes in the morning.

The light burns into your dreams
And you strain to see clearly
Once you wake.

Such a stark contrast
To the long stretch of darkness.

SUNSET PT. 2

As the day creeps to its end,
As the sun starts to bend,
Lowering itself to sleep,
I am calm.

No, this isn't the end.
This is a goodnight.
I'll see you again.
I've survived the day,
And I'll survive the next.

OPEN HEART

Doors were closed,
Hallways seemed too long,
Stairs kept going and going,
So I felt stuck.

But suddenly everything feels like an opportunity
Where the turns in a maze
Lead to bright new revelations
And every doorway offers a room full of flowers.

I thought about hiding away my heart,
But it is open and now it is full
And I feel so much more alive.

YOU LOOK AT ME

If I open my eyes
And see you staring at me
The way that you do,
I feel myself opening up,
Unfolding like a blooming flower.

You are sunlight,
And I love to bask in your warmth.

TELL ME THIS

You are amazing.
You have a good heart.
You are wonderful.
You create beautiful art.
You are brave.
You have always been this.
You are resilient.
You have nothing to miss.
You are better as you are now.

HEALING

I know I am better
When your love isn't what keeps me alive.

It is no longer the raft on the open sea.

I am afloat in shallow water on my own,
staring into sunny blue skies.

TO MY BODY

I have not always been kind to it,
Not cherishing it, protecting it,
Or treating it like it's beautiful.

And I am sorry how I have failed
And how that self-hatred prevailed.
Not any longer. Not anymore.

This is my body, the only one I own,
And there should be love shown.
Though it may not be perfect or ideal
To today's standards of beauty or sex appeal,
It is deserving of kindness,
Of gentleness, of adoration,
As am I.

LINES AND CURVES

The shape of me had always been disappointing. I was never what I wanted to be. I was never enough of what was the ideal beauty of the time. I was the wrong colour, and came from the wrong place, and didn't have the right thing. I was out of place and unnoticed and cruel to myself.

I am tired of that. I am tired and I am done. I am ready to unlearn the cruelty and learn how to be kind. I want to be loving and sweet. I want to be caring and gentle. I want to kiss my own cuts and speak the words I need to hear instead of waiting for someone else to do so.

I am not lines or curves. I am not the colour of my eyes or the softness of my hair. I am not the state of my skin, the smoothness or the supposed imperfections. I am not the shape of my lips or the size of my hands. I am not the dress I'm wearing or the sweater that hides me. I am more than a body, than a heart, than a life.

I am more than what I thought I was. I am much more important. I am something unique and shining and special. I am something to love, something to cherish. I am something that matters in the endless universe we exist within. I am not just a person, but my own individual. I am like no one else and I should be adored for that.

I am dusted in glitter and flaws and I am so, so worthy regardless of what I've believed of myself in the days before.

ISN'T IT ROMANTIC?

The most romantic thing I can do
Is shower myself with affection.
Isn't it romantic how I smile at myself,
How my reflection and I laugh together
Like we share private jokes and good memories,
Like there is so much to enjoy in life?

Isn't it romantic to have someone
Look at you and gasp at your beauty?
And better yet, isn't it romantic
If that person is you? Yourself?
Only you know what you need
And how love should proceed
To ensure you feel treasured.

Love is not easy.
To love yourself may be harder.
But isn't romantic when you do?

THE LIGHT

When the world feels dark and empty,
I look to you to find the light.

You are not the sun,
Not a flashlight or a match.
You are the one waiting
At the end of the tunnel,
A reminder of what's waiting for me
When I escape the darkness.

The brightness,
The joy,
The relief,
The light
That you are.

WITH YOU

Pardon me
For this epiphany,
But I believe
That what I perceive
Is something real,
Something true,
Something a lot like love
With you.

SOMEONE ELSE

My mother hates that I've felt I needed another person to feel valued. She hates that I've sought attention from people who don't deserve my time. She hates that I've cried over people who couldn't provide the love I craved and how desperately I desired their affection.

I want her to be proud of me, to see me laughing on my own because I can make myself happy. I want her to listen to me ramble with excitement about what I can do on my own. I want to make her proud and bring her joy. I want to be a reason she smiles, rather than making her cry. I want to be strong enough to carry her when it becomes necessary, as she carried me when I fell to my knees and wept.

She is so strong, so independent, so brave. She is much wiser and older than me, bolder than me, and knows how I should be treated. She knows that I don't need a man to make my heart light up, that a man isn't necessary to move forward in life, that a man could hold me back instead of urging me ahead. She knows I should not tolerate less than adoration and hates when I allow anything mediocre into my life.

I am exceptional, beautiful, bright. I am a glowing thing all on my own and sometimes I might not see it, but my mother always does. I am the light to lead myself out of the dark. I am the one with the candle and the match and hands to hold it all.

If I ever need someone else, the only one I need is her. She is the reminder to move towards being self-sufficient and discovering self-love. I hope to have her strength, to be worthy of her love. I hope that she knows if I needed anyone else, it's someone like her.

YOUR LOVE

It matters and helps create a picture,
But it is not the only thing I see.
Your love is a patch of light
But I am my own sun.
I illuminate the world on my own.

Instead, you are like the stars.

You are beautiful and enduring.
You are there even when I cannot see you.
You bring some shine to the darkness.

VERSUS MINE

The love I feel for myself
Is the thing that holds together
The panes of coloured stained glass
In the window of a grand cathedral.

Self-love makes sense of my life
And allows me to see the beauty of it.

KISS THIS

You won't find the wounds on me anymore.
But I'll let you try to look for them.
I'll let you press a kiss here and there.
As if I'm still in agony
And your affection is a remedy.

SIMPLY THIS

Sometimes you are gentle,
Sometimes you are rough,
But I always know with you,
I am much more than simply enough.

WHAT YOU INSPIRE

I am not very musical by nature,
but you inspire a song in me.
The melody is bright and delightful,
The lyrics as romantic as I've ever been.

You make me shine with this adoration,
This marvelousness that makes me laugh
So much that it feels like I am a fountain
Of joy, of warmth, of bubbles and sugar.

I am not very bold or strong.
But you inspire bravery and strength in me.
Anything seems possible,
Everything within my reach.

What you inspire are dreams that come true,
And all you've offered is a sanctuary
Only for me and for you.

IF YOU WANT ME

External validation doesn't keep me alive. It doesn't keep my heart beating or ensure my lungs work as they should. It doesn't smooth out my breaths or calm the tension in my body. It doesn't hold my hand or cradle me to their chest in the dead of night when thoughts speed through my mind like a racetrack crowded with cars revving their engines so loud that they drown out the rest of the world. Those thoughts spin out of control and it is an inevitable accident, a disaster that cannot be stopped. All you can do is wait it out. Sometimes that's all I need: to wait.

External validation does not keep me going. Kind words and soft kisses won't erase my scars. Your promises won't stop any bleeding. You cannot patch up a broken heart with band-aids. You cannot heal me.

But if you want me, act like it. Shower me with love like petals drifting down from the branches of cherry blossom trees on a bright, breezy spring day. Let me feel it like the sun on my skin after weeks of artificial light while we've been stuck in quarantine, kept apart like we exist on the opposite sides of an ocean.

Tell me I'm on your mind and I'm in your heart, not like a scar but like a patch over the rips and tears of the people who hurt you before we met each other. A bit of stitching that won't close the wound but will do plenty to help it heal right. Tell me that I came to you in your dreams like the ethereal ghost of a future lover, a promise on my lips that everything will be okay. Let me learn that you want to be holding me against you, stroking my hair and whispering into my ear that you will be here, that you'll take care of me, that it feels right to be together.

Because, if you don't, I won't believe that this thing is real. I won't feel safe when we're apart. I won't want to put any effort into brightening your days when you're barely peeking into mine like it's a room you've entered a few times but were too daunted to visit again. I won't insist on making something work if the other pieces of the machine won't even bother to play their roles. I won't try to breathe life into this creature of a relationship, letting it die if you won't take turns to keep it alive.

If you cannot appreciate me, if you cannot assure me of your wanting, of your heart desiring to entwine with mine, then I won't allow myself the hurt. The aching that comes from wanting to be yours but not having it will be a thing buried in a chest adorned in locks with long-lost keys sunk beneath ocean waves in the lowest depths. I'll leave it there and focus my mind and body and being into something of greater value. Of something that values me the way you may not. The way you have failed to accomplish.

I do enough hurting without doubting you. I do enough aching without wondering if you are aching for me too in the hours and days and weeks and months we spend apart. Every day is a vast journey to embark upon and I make it in hopes of meeting you halfway. I cannot make it alone. I cannot take the steps only to realize that you haven't even turned in my direction.

Don't plant false hope into me like a seed in cement. It cannot grow, but it's there, perhaps trying to catch light through the holes left by bubbles. Don't let me water something that's destined to die, to never flourish beyond the speck. It's a discarded opportunity that perhaps had no chance of ever existing. Don't do that to me. I deserve more. I deserve better than that, no matter how much I've been drawn to you all this time. How much more hurt I've allowed into my life.

I don't need external validation, so I won't seek it out. I won't ask you to stretch your limbs when you'd prefer to lay still. I'm strong enough to stand on my own two feet, to push myself when I'm tired. I hold onto my determination like a walking stick that keeps me steady as I hike through a trailway I've forged myself in a dense forest. I can keep myself alive with slow, steady breaths in a soothing pattern I've learned throughout years of discovering and developing coping strategies. Those are things I've collected like treasure, hoarding them in my heart and mind like it's more valuable than diamonds and gold.

There's no need for me to rely on someone else to remind me that I should keep trying to remain afloat despite churning waves threatening to drag me under the surface. On my own, I can remember that I still know how to tread water, that I know how to cough to clear my lungs, that breathing comes naturally so long as I can stay calm.

I don't need someone else to call me beautiful and brilliant when I already know that to be true. When I see myself in the mirror and find the love that matters most: the love I have for me.

If you want me, offer that or more. If you want me, I shouldn't have to convince myself that you might. If you want me, remember that I don't need you to hold me up. I can stand steady without your aid that I haven't asked for. If you want me, act like it. If you want me, shower me in love like flower petals. Let me never know a day of darkness. Let every blink of the eye be nothing more than a flash of a moment in the shadows. If you want me, make me feel like love is endless. Make it feel attainable. Make it mine and yours and ours.

But don't ever think that I won't survive without anyone's love. I have my own. That will keep me alive. I've found it like it's the fountain of youth, long hunted but finally within my grasp. I have it and cherish it and though sometimes I may misplace it, I will always find it again.

I don't need anyone else, but if you want me, prove that we're something worth fighting for. If you want me, show me that you believe we have something good, something we should keep alive. Show me that you see value in it. In us. In this sanctuary we could build together.

FOR MYSELF

Growing up
And getting older
It's not just my bones
Or my brain taking on the years.

I feel my youth at its strongest
When words spill out of my mouth,
Out of control and chaotic.
I'm learning to rein them in,
To put a leash on my nonsense
And say only what should be said.

Words can be weaponized.
Keep your voice guarded.

UNDER THE PILLOW

I have learned to keep myself safe
By placing a knife under my pillow
And holding a vial of poison beneath my tongue.
It's dangerous to myself and others,
A toss of dice of who will be hurt.

A risk we take to keep myself sane
To know I am doing what I can
Even if it's a little intense.

THE BRIDGE

The place where I am
And where I need to be
Is connected by a frayed rope bridge.

It's coming undone and swaying
Over the deep drop between the cliffs
And yet still
I cross
Terrified
Trembling

Because I have to get there
To be better than who I was.

BREATHING TECHNIQUES

One of the things I need to survive is
breathing the right way.

My lungs work fine,
A diaphragm that contracts and expands
But without the ease there should be.
Fear makes them struggle
So fear had to be handled.

You do it with counting
With patterns
With filling a box
Closing your eyes
And just breathing
As best as you can
Until you are better.

And I am. I'm here. I'm breathing.
That's the first step.

HOW TO COPE

There are different methods for different days,
For the variety of issues I'll have to face.
There are symptoms I can catalogue
And ways to relieve the discomfort.

Sometimes
The usual medicine fails
And while I ail,
I need to find
That perfect antidote
For the fresh poison
In my mind.

Every time I descend
Into that dark place,
I must remember
There is a remedy
And soon I'll be me
Again.

THE TOOLBOX

- a box to fill
- pills and more pills
- a shoulder to cry on
- a notebook to write on
- a long nap during the day
- a playlist that knows what to say
- endless embraces
- quiet rooms as safe places
- the purrs of my cat
- exercises on my yoga mat
- and the knowledge that I can conquer this

AS THE DOCTOR SAYS

If one method fails,
Try another.

We can figure this out.
You will get through this.

There are many ways
Out of the abyss.

LIKE BEFORE

Hey, remember how weird it felt
To suddenly wake
Without that deep ache?

How eternal it had seemed
Until all that you dreamed
Of being happy
And carefree
Came true?

That place was cruel
But you got unstuck
And it wasn't luck
That led you home.

It was you
And love
And care
And there,
Before you know it,
The hurt was in the past.
So it happens but it won't last.

Like before,
You can get through this.
You can do this.

Like before,
You survived.
You are alive.

BLAME GAME

We used to play this game
Of who gets the blame.

These days, I've drained away the hate.
Replaced it with kindness and courage,
With the realization that I did it.

I won the battle.
I vanquished demons.

FAIRY TALE

I want to live in a fairy tale world
Where the flowers bloom bigger
And brighter at my touch,
The castle that's my home
Enchanted to keep me safe.

And you
Looking at me like I'm a wonder,
Always believing the best of me
No matter how much of the worst
You've witnessed.

Lucky me
To have a romantic heart
That makes me believe
All of this is an option.

DAMSEL

Nothing wrong with needing a little love,
An outstretched hand to help you up.
I've been down, been brittle and shattered.
But I wasn't a damsel in distress.
I didn't need a knight in shining armour.
I needed my own army, my own shield and sword.

So I forged my own.

PRINCESS THE TOWER

There was a monster that kept me chained,
Locked away in a dark room away
From anyone who could save the day.

I was alone in the shadows,
Shaking in shackles,
Wondering when I'd finally be free.

I had to believe in me,
To learn new things in order to be
Able to live and love without fear.

MIRROR

Our eyes meet and I know the truth:
You are so resilient and strong,
Coming such a long way
Down a difficult path.
And I am so proud of you.

Love is hard but I am certain
That you can find it for yourself.
That you will have it.
That you deserve it
And only the best kind.

STITCHES

The healing can hurt
Like the needle that sews stitches.

Take the pain now.
The little pinpricks of it.

It's merely part of the process.

RAINBOW

Have you ever tried to follow the rainbow?
Chasing the arch as it hangs over you in the sky
With your head filled with images of paradise
So long as you can follow the path before it fades away.

Happiness felt like that,
Trying to reach for a rainbow like it's a rope
That will lead me somewhere beautiful and better
Than the stormy state of my world.
A temporary option that I could never really hold.

Now I know better,
A rainbow will disappear
When there's no sun during a storm.
Later, it will come back.

Happiness is like that too.
When your heart is grey and your head is cloudy,
The rare moments of joy are the most exciting
And though they seem fleeting,
You can count on them to come again.

RED RED RED

Teach me to be bold.
I am tired of being afraid
And yet that's all I feel
When I look at you.
The good kind, the one of the heart
When it runs and races
And reminds me that I'm alive.

You're wonderful and bright
And my face is red red red
Because all I can think about is kissing you.
My lips are stained
From those lucky moments.
Remnants of shyness,
Blushing red,
Bolder with you.

ORANGE SUNSET

When you chase beauty and the best moments,
You find gold stars against midnight blue,
Bright yellow against baby blue skies
and snow-white clouds,
And somewhere in between

The warm glow as the light descends
and the dark creeps out,
When day and night kiss for a few seconds
And their embrace is bright orange.

EVERYTHING YELLOW

The sky was grey, but my world was yellow,
Painted with broad strokes of sunlight
As remnants of my best days.
The bad ones become nothing more than clouds
Blown away once I catch my breath.

ENVY GREEN

This is better than feeling like I have no light in me.
At least this way I have a glow,
One that is unkind and selfish.

I won't apologize for all this green
Even if it doesn't look good on me.
Know that it comes from a secret place
That I've tried to protect and hide away.
You found your way through the gates
And made yourself home here in my heart.

So forgive me for this envy,
Wishing I could have all this time with you
And make the rest of the world wait instead.

BLUE FOR NOW

The wide expanse of sky
Reminds me of the reasons why
I should always keep going.

I might be blue,
Light and hopeful and bright,
Or I might be drenched in midnight,
Dark and uncertain and frightening.
But the sky flits between the shades
From pale to dark to bright to night.
Time passes and it might seem slow,
Yet it can be filled with beautiful things to know.

There are many adventures within this one
To explore and enjoy in life, not death,
And so I should wait for the sun
That rises every day.

It will clear the darkness
And everything will be okay.

INDIGO

There have been so many wrong turns,
I don't know where the paths are anymore.

Now you hold my hand,
Leading me through a labyrinth.
I close my eyes and let us go.

We'll end up in a bookstore,
Staring up at the shelves
And stuck in our dreams.

How did you know this was home?
That this is where I feel safe?
All I know are wonders here,
Daydreams and starlight and
All things astonishing.

VIOLETS

I did not want to write of romance
Or of opening up to this chance
Filled with longing and quick glances
And wondering how I'm held in your heart.

But I've since decided to hold on
To the details that keep me warm,
From the way you meet my eyes,
To your calm embrace during an emotional storm.

I don't need fancy bouquets or even
A handful of wildflowers and weeds.
I don't care if the petals are pin or violet,
Or if you've got nothing but a handful of green.

All I want is a quiet moment with you,
Sitting together and realizing what's true:
That one could ever matter as much as you do.

SLOWER

Louder people look in love with life,
Moving fast and never staying still,
As if they can never have their fill.

Sometimes I wish I was like them,
Racing through the days in a rush
But it's different when every single brush
With imperfection leaves me stuttering,
Stumbling, knocked far off balance.

So maybe it's okay
To traverse a little slower.
I enjoy my days relaxed and easy,
And I'm content with myself today.

THE APOTHECARY

Here you will find
Many things to alter your mind.
There are shelves bearing glasses and vials
And rose-scented romance in the aisles.

Beware of the labels
That some have replaced
To mask their malice
And appeal to your senses.
Beware their smiles and false pretences.
All the luck in the universe
Will not save you from a curse
Of someone with a heart of stone.

FRESH AIR

There are days when all I need
Is an open window offering sunlight
And the knowledge that I can breathe deep
Then go right back to sleep.

The brightness burns my eyes,
But my heartbeat is slow and steady,
Happy to know that I can go on
Whenever I am ready.

ANTIDOTE

The truth is that some people are sweet poison.
Once you have a taste, you cannot stop.
Kiss after kiss, they kill you slowly,
Letting you believe you're their one and only.

Though I have no need of a hero,
It soothes me to know
That I will not face anything alone.
Perhaps the cure is a call on the phone.
Your soft voice will awaken me
When the sleep that's taken me,
And I'll come back to the world of the living.

No, I don't need someone to save me,
Or someone to care for me gently.
It is simply sweet to know
That your embrace is the place to go
When I need healing.

Or maybe you're not a cure.
Maybe you're my armour.

TRYING TO BE GOOD

My mind always focuses on the teachings
From my school days and all the readings
About life and death, heaven and hell,
Good and bad and all in the middle.

I try to remember
That after September
I have the chance
To sing and dance
And celebrate being me.

I might not always be good
And don't behave as I should,
But I know I deserve love
And joy and peace.

Because I am trying
In the very least.

HOLY THINGS

What makes things better than others?
It's how we see them, how we treat them,
How we decide to spread our love.

The things that are holy to me
Are not always things you can see.
It's the friendships I've kept,
The support received when I wept,
The apologies accepted,
The people I've affected,
And the fact I'm not alone.

PRAYERS

In my darkest hours,
I could not find God.

I spoke my prayers,
Whispered them into the night.
And found no help in sight.

The difference is
These days I keep trying,
Keep whispering my prayers,
And waiting for answers,
With hope in my heart.

FORGIVE ME

Asking for forgiveness
Leaves me in a sickness.
It hurts to realize what I've done
And who I've hurt however I did.

On my worst days,
I hold onto these mistakes,
Keeping the pieces of all I break,
And cutting myself with the shards.

But I'm learning to say sorry,
To acknowledge my failure,
To fix what I broke,
To keep you and me.

LITTLE THINGS

I learned something new
About what I can do
To make each day more bearable.

All I have to do is hold on
To the tiny bits of life that make
The terrible things much easier to take.

BIRDS PT. 2

If I were a bird,
I'd had broken wings.
Bandages wrapped around them now,
And I'd have a new, hopeful song to sing.

If I were a bird,
I'd know I could fly again.
That sometimes it will get dark
But the sun still shines after rain.

SWEET TOOTH

They might not be the healthiest things
And perhaps I could survive without them.
I know what my mouth craves,
The rush that my body desires,
The crystals on my tongue.

My sweet tooth is reliable,
A little thing that enables
Me to last another day longer
With a mouthful of sugar
To make me feel stronger.

It seems silly to those who don't know
That searching for a treat
Gives me somewhere to go.
It gets me out of bed
And that awful place in my head
In hopes of a spark of joy.

SUGAR RUSH

What I need to get going
Is a little thing to survive the day
With the kind of sweetness
That leads to tooth decay.

I need that flash of energy.
The burst of life and joy.
It seems so childish and silly
But the sugar on my tongue
And the rush that comes with it
Makes it easier to tolerate all of life's shit.

SMALL MOMENTS

It takes an hour, a second, a minute, or more,
To make a day turn from bad to good to better.
It could be curling under a blanket
Or getting cozy in a new, warm sweater.
It could be dancing to a song linked with laughter,
Maybe ending a long day by reading a book chapter.
Sometimes it's finding chocolates I've hidden,
The relief from finishing some time at the gym,
Or the knowledge that I get an evening with him.

There are little moments,
Small things that seem like nothing,
But they all add up to feeling alive,
Making me feel like I can handle anything.

CLUTCHING

My hands couldn't grasp anything for a while,
But now I'm holding on tightly
To the things that make me smile.

I'm clutching handfuls
Of flowers and ice cream cones,
Of pictures of loved ones.
I'm clutching onto you,
Our fingers entwined,
Knowing your presence
Can give me peace of mind.

LIFE JACKET

There are days when what I need is a hug,
A warm embrace
In which I bury my face
Against a strong, steady shoulder.

With some arms around me,
I feel safe and happy,
And know that I can go on.

Those arms could be my life jacket,
The thing keeping my head above water,
The grip to assist me when I am weary.
Still, I tread, and having you with me
Reminds me that I have nothing to fear.

FLOATING

I am floating on.
I am surviving.
Sometimes
That's enough.

DEEP BREATHS

Inhale, exhale.
I have to be okay.
Inhale, exhale.
Take it day by day.
Inhale, exhale.

HAND-HOLDING

If we just sit here,
Our hands together,
All is easier.

Like this,
You are my anchor.

TETHERED

Sometimes I drift away from the real world.
I've learned that's the warning sign.
When that begins to happen,
I have to search for something to hold,
To remember to be in the moment
Instead of inside my head.

Before my mind can wander,
I grab the edges of reality,
Knot it around my wrists,
So that when I descend
Into that dark place,
I can pull myself out of it again.

YOUR WORDS

No one realizes how much a word can mean,
how much a single one can change the scene.
The right words can clear a dark, stormy sky,
Or offer warmth in the middle of winter.

Your words are the ones I need you to say.
The sweet ones, the soft ones,
The ones that calm and soothe and comfort.

FIRST

The lesson that sticks with me
Is that in order to be happy,
I have to remember who comes first.

To rely on others for happiness
Is to be unbalanced and unsure.
Caring for myself is the only cure.

I have to take care of myself
Before I look for anyone else.
To tell myself that I am loved
By my very own heart.
To look at myself and feel lovely
Without someone else to tell me.

I am my own protector.

SELF-CARE

Every day, I need something different.
Healing doesn't happen the same every time.
Maybe I need to sleep a little longer.
Tomorrow I might need to chase the sun.
I could even dance alone for a bit of fun.

Self-care doesn't always look the same.
I discover new methods every day.

THIS NEVER HAPPENED

1.   I fell in love in the middle of a pandemic. Closed doors, locked windows, songs and screams from balconies. I risked it all for a boy with soft lips and a gentle heart and no time at all for me. I fell in love in the middle of a quarantine, sneaking through the streets to steal a few kisses from someone I'd love forever. These were months of intensity, of insanity, of knowing that the end was a long way ahead. We were twisting around each other, making promises in the breaths between our mouths, when we came up for air and somehow had an endless list of things to say. I fell in love in the middle of death and chaos and grief and danger. I found hope in my romantic heart and dreams about better days that would be much different than   the   days   we   had   before.

2.   I think I stood on the roof at two in the morning, wrapped in a parka because my body could not stop shaking even though the days were getting warmer and the end of the isolation was approaching. But all I could see was the ground below me, several stories away from me. I swayed during these early hours and held onto this realization that I am alive alive alive and I could so easily be dead. Here I am, inches from toppling from the edge of the world into a violent abyss but I keep my feet planted and set my breaths even. I am unsteady but I am still standing and I am still going. I am still. I am here. I stand

at the edge of the rooftop and I think I can step back into
my   home.

3.   I laid in a bed that wasn't mine and curled the
blankets around me like this would be my new home. It
smells like a man who doesn't know my heart in its
entirety yet, but he dearly wishes to. He isn't in here with
me, off to the bathroom to wash his face and scrub at his
skin. I think my hair will stain his pillow with the scent of
jasmine from my perfume and the oils I stroke into the
strands for softness. When I turn my head to bury my face
against his sheets, I sigh and wonder if I will fall in love
with him. If I'll remember this night as something
beautiful instead of something sad. I came here because I
was lonely. I came here because my heart was empty and
I wanted to fill it with someone's temporary love. When I
leave in the morning, neither he nor I will know if this
night meant anything more than filling the gaps.

4.   There are new love letters on my bedside table and
none of them have a name on them. Some are for me,
others for people I don't really know. People I've sent
messages in which I've made myself bare and vulnerable,
like tilting my head to expose my throat to a bloodthirsty
beast. I think one of those letters talks about that, naming
the beast Romance. Romance is cruel and far-fetched. It's
the leopard a child thinks it might find in their background
forest. Romance is a phantom scar you haven't yet found

on your skin, but it's inevitable. Romance is a beast of teeth and talons and it knows how to slide between your ribs to get to your heart. It knows how to kiss, to caress, to squeeze and squeeze and squeeze. I think these love letters should be burned and set into the sky like fireworks. I think I'll keep them a secret because while I recognize myself as a hopeless romantic, that isn't always who I want   to   be.

5.   I live in daydreams. It's how I get through slow afternoons and nights that stretch too long. I create new worlds and new scenarios where my heart soars or maybe it aches. Maybe I cling to moments that are so overwhelming with emotion, that I forget when I am laying around with my eyes wide open and the real world existing in a blur. When my muscles are numb and my tongue is glued to the roof of my mouth. If I can have nothing else, at least I have my imagination.

THIS ROMANTIC IN ME

In the lonely hours that exist during weeks in isolation,
I reached out to too many people and not enough.
There is something new in the way I've stretched myself,
These limbs, this tongue, this heart that doesn't know
How to stay still when it doesn't know where it belongs.

The romantic part of me might be worse
than my anxiety,
Worse than the demon that is my depression
on the worst days.
It's a wicked thing that tells me to
dream and dream and dream
Until I'm drifting off in the middle of an endless ocean.

I cannot fathom a world where I do not hope
as much as I do now.
The things I conjure in my mind are like bear traps,
And when I find them, I still knowingly step into them.
The agony is expected and yet it's what I want.
It's somehow
Satisfying.

And part of me wonders if the romantic in me
Is more violent than the knives
I'd dragged across my wrists,
Sharper than the razors I used to scratch at my waist.
I think this part of me is awful and

I need to curb the habit.

This is a curse and a cure.
I wish for love. I want it all around me.

All of its joys and all its dangers.

Maybe I should be afraid,
But I don't know if I've ever been this brave.

TREMBLING

There are no scars.
My mind is quiet.

The only remnants
Of where I went
Are my shaking hands.

I am trembling
Like I'm still at the edge of a cliff.

At least it doesn't hurt.

STRONGER

My body is stronger.
My heart is healed.
I'm not just afloat;
I'm crossing an ocean.

AFTERWARDS

When you have lived in the dark,
I hope that it's made you kinder.
Come equipped with flashlights
And rope and water and all the skills
You need to survive.

And if you find someone else
In that dark hole you fell into before,
You'll be there to show them the way out.

STILL DOUBTING

Despite how far I've travelled on this journey,
I still wonder if I'm going the right way.

STILL UNSTEADY

My body has new muscles,
All knotted with memories.
I can stand and walk and run.
But there are days when I fall
And I wonder if I'm still too weak.

I'm stronger these days,
But still a little unsteady.

STILL SCARED

Bravery always felt so far-fetched.
A shooting star I'd never catch,
A feather floating far above and away.

Maybe I've faced the demons before,
Learned how to evade the bites and bruising.
But when I am staring down the mouth of the beast,
I'll still be afraid.

I still wonder if I'll survive it.

LET ME SLEEP

Can I stay here?
Can I lay my head down?
Can you hold me when I wake
And speak softly to me until I fall back asleep?

Can I hold onto this quiet, safe feeling?

GOOD DREAMS

The nightmares had faded to fog.
Haunting words and relentless worries
Turning into nothing more than wisps.

I'm not dreaming of anyone
Or imagining some lovely little place.
I'm not dreaming of better days
Or losing myself in fantasies.

I have good dreams now,
The kind where I can float,
Where I can rest,
Where I can simply
exist.

EPIC

There is nothing epic in my life
Except that I am alive.

That is the adventure.

REALITY

There is a place in the world that I can claim as my own. It's painted in pastels and rainbows where there are arches. It smells like sunshine and lilacs and there are chocolate-tasting bubbles floating in the air. A gentle breeze ruffles the delicate leaves of swaying willows and it's a comfortable sort of warmth, not the one that makes your skin slick and sticky with sweat, but that kind that makes you sigh in a soft sort of satisfaction.

I think this place is laid out like a picnic with enough plush velvet pillows to lay across like I have made the most comfortable bed. We are spread out on the grass with brown summer skin, our limbs splayed out like we were caught in the middle of making angels. There is a garden nearby that is fresh-smelling and full of flowers at the peak of their bloom. Someone nearby is playing a romantic melody on a grand piano that drifts towards us like it's carried by the wind that wants everyone to close their eyes and just listen, just exist, in a calm sort of bliss.

It seems dreamlike, this bit of the world. It seems like I've pieced together some of my favourite things and maybe I have. The part that strikes me as something sensational is the fact that these things exist in their own ways and I could have the different fragments scattered across multiple moments and I could still keep them with me when I needed some time to find my peace.

I am dreamy. I am romantic. I have this part of the world that doesn't exist this way all the time but it could and that possibility settles a song around my heart like ribbons wrapped around a silvery present. It makes me laugh and smile. It is not real all the time but it could be real. It could be mine.

It seems silly to search for this dream somewhere in the world.

But if I keep thinking I can find it, I can be okay.

THE STICKY BITS

You can see where I've been wounded.
You can see the injuries that have now healed.
You can see the outline of band-aids,
The sticky bits left over from where they were.

You can see where I'd been cut.
You can see where I'd bled.
You can see that I patched myself up,
That I wanted to stop the hurting.

You can see that I knew pain.
You can see that I healed again
And again and again.

You can see where I laid the band-aids,
The sticky bits that stayed
Even when I didn't need to cover up anymore.

SWING SET

My favourite part of the park is the swing set.
Watch me kick my legs, stretch my feet to the sky.
I'll tip my head back and laugh so loud
The other kids will look my way.

Watch me reach for the clouds,
Racing towards them like I can fly.
I'll stay here forever, or at least until sunset.

I'm weightless like this,
Unburdened by gravity.

I am happy like this,
Unaffected by the rest of the world.

CAROUSEL

Round and round we go,
Again and again and again,
Until we're dizzy with delight.

Merry-go-round,
Marry me here.

Keep me in this moment in time
That lets me be so carefree.
I'll tilt my head back
And close my eyes
As the music plays along.

Take a picture of me here.
Let's remember this day.
Let's go round and round and round,
Before it gets dark, while the light remains.

HAND KISSES

Take my hand to your lips,
Press a kiss there before I slip
Away from you and to the dark,
Where I won't remember the feeling
Of the moments we could be stealing.

Take my hand and lead my away
So I won't wander off and stay
Somewhere you can't come too
And I can't figure out what's true.

Take my hand and kiss me there
To remind me of how much you care
Because sometimes I'll forget why
Exactly I shouldn't want to die
When I can be right here,
With you always near.

Take my hand and kiss it softly.
Take my hand and promise me
That we can have this every day

And it isn't just a game to play.

Take my hand
And help me stand.

COTTON CANDY

When the sky is blue and the clouds are pink,
When there is sugar in my mouth
And a laugh spilling across my tongue.
When everything is sweet and bright,
When I feel young and alive,
And nothing else matters.

I want my life to be like cotton candy,
Light and sweet and full of colour.
I want my life to be this lovely.

BLISSED OUT

Look at me, lying here beside you.
Eyes closed, smile on my lips.
I think my body is worn out.
I think my heart is finally slowing.

I think you press a kiss to my forehead
Before I close my eyes and cuddle close.
Can you feel me relax against you?
Do you know where I've gone?

I'm somewhere in the corner of my mind,
Trying to memorize every detail of this moment.
I'm blissed out in this daydream,
This perfect piece of time.

PILL BOX

Every day, I flip open the lid.
Deep breath, deep sigh,
Better than wanting to die.

I count them out like stars in the city's night sky,
Make sure I've got the right amount, not too high,
Not too little, just enough so I can lie
In bed, mind clear and body calm.

MEDICATED

I am stretched across the sandy ground,
The sun relentlessly hot against my skin.
My muscles were all rope unwound.
There's a bit of a burn on my body
But this is so much better than it's been.

I smell the sea in the air,
The salt of it clinging to my hair.
I think about where I was only weeks ago
And how I thought I'd never know this place,
This peace.

HANDS FULL

One, two, three, four.
For my mind, my body, my pain.
One, two, three, four,
A bunch to keep me sane.

I'm proud, entirely free of shame
that I take these little things.
They ensure I'm no longer the same
person who hurt so much.

I take them to be whole,
To find the person the illness stole.
To be me again, to see myself in the mirror.

HAZY

Lazy, hazy, not so crazy.
Feeling weightless,
Feeling like I could fly.

It used to feel like I was sinking,
But now I'm ready to soar.

MAYBE MAYBE MAYBE

For this moment,
I want to share a secret.
My heart has been bitter and cold.
I have known more anger than ever.
Hatred has never rung deep in me,
And yet it was something I was learning.

Then you come along,
Come back into my life,
And show me again what it is like
To be filled with yearning.

I am all eagerness, all excitement.
The world is filled with wonder.
Maybe it's being with you,
Maybe it's just being better.
Maybe this is how it's supposed to be.

STARLIGHT

When the first star winks in the sky,
I think about how I made it through another day.
Since the first time I found myself in the dark,
Things have changed.

I look for the first glimpse of light
When the dark comes during the night.
Some joy emerges when I am afraid.
Something that fills my heart to the top,
That makes me remember what I love about life.

This world is beautiful and I want to stay in it.
I want to look for the hope that glimmers and glitters
Just like the stars in the night sky.

They don't illuminate the sky,
But the little things still mean a lot.

CONSTELLATIONS

Star to star, dot to dot,
If you connect them,
You'll discover stories.

Each shape has one.
Each story has value.
And every star has a name.

People are like that too:
Bright on our own,
Connected to others,
With our own stories to share.

UNDER THE MOON

There was a night
When we sat in the dark.
The moon emerged from the clouds
And climbed up the sky.

It had a hazy, orange glow,
Stark in contrast to the shadows.
The beauty of it struck me silent
And I wondered if I was like this:
Bright against the dark,
Beautiful in my ascent.

OPEN WATER

Nothing but a rope separates me from this boardwalk
and the open water.
When the sun hangs low and the night draws closer,
I used to wonder
What if would be like if I stepped over the edge
and fell under?
The water is cold and still and uncertain.

But there's no temptation like that in me this evening.
Those thoughts were anvils chained to my ankles,
the links now snapped.
The prison of such bleak ideas has opened
all the windows and doors.
Fresh air hits me all at once like
I'm at the docks or the pier
Or that boardwalk on the edge of the city
that overlooks the lake.

I have seen different views across the open water.
I have felt different things at different times
over the years.
But the open water is less like a siren
and more like a reminder
That I have stood here so many times
and it's never quite the same
Except for one thing.

It's always been beautiful.

SUNSETS ON THE LAKE

It's lovely to look at the lake
When the sun heads to sleep
And I can sit at the edge of the water
In absolute silence.

No cruel monster in my head,
No wishing to be dead.
Nothing more than the fact
That this view is always astonishing.

NOISE

What shocked me most on the path to recovery was the lack of noise. I hadn't realized I'd been in a cavern that echoed endlessly. No one told me that this was how it was supposed to be, that the rest of the people in this world could exist without someone screaming at them all the time. No one warned me that there would be so much noise on the worst days and so much quiet on the best. It's like trying to sleep but your neighbours keep banging the doors and getting into fights so loud it scrapes their throats hoarse. That it feels like your eyes are closed but someone is prying them open and shining their brightest flashlights into them. That when you could sleep at night with white noise and absolute dark and your body settles into peace because it's time to rest.

You could lay in silence, hear nothing but your own heart and the slowing of your breaths. You could close your eyes and you would be left unbothered, allowed to relax. That you could simply be without feeling like something bad will happen when you are vulnerable. That you could drift through life without aches and pains that are born in the anger and dread built up by your traitorous mind.

I didn't know I could have silence. I didn't know it could be so peaceful. I feel like I can finally sleep and there wouldn't be nightmares waiting for me.

PARANOIA

The goosebumps are gone now.
The shivers have slowed to stillness.
Paranoia is a thing of the past.

I am braver now,
Safe even on my own.
Free of fears and tears.

LOOK BACK

I know it's a good day
When I'm not expecting anyone to say
That I'm going to crash into chaos.

I know it's a good day
When I can go my own way
Without wondering if anybody
Is following me.

I know it's a good day
When I don't look back
Like I'm expecting an attack.

FEELING SAFE

Doors unlocked, windows without bars,
Eyes closed as we dance with our arms in the air.
Sleeping with my back to the door,
Walking without my eyes wandering away.
Chasing you knowing I'll catch up,
Waiting but knowing you'll be back soon.

I like the softness of this,
The security, the safety,
The fact that I'll be okay.

WALKING ALONE

Something that used to scare me was walking alone. I would look over my shoulder, hurry ahead, thoughts running through my mind as if there was someone always behind. I felt like I was being chased by demons that intended on herding me to hell. Everything seemed so awful. It felt like that was the only way to go.

These days, I can feel a bit of the breeze. It brushes against my cheek and ruffles my hair. I don't flinch when someone walks close. I don't run like I'm in a race. When I walk, I don't mind being alone. There's music in my ears and things to do. There's something like hope curled around me like a shield from any incoming danger. I think I'm not so afraid of the city anymore.

I don't ask for a hand to hold.
I don't shake as I'm walking alone.
I think I can do this.
I think I'm learning how to carry on.

NEW TATTOOS

Let's keep it simple.
Clean lines, some shadows,
Distinct images that say
Who I've become today.

If I ever forget what matters,
All I have to do is look at my skin.
There are memories in ink now,
Reminders of the people I love,
And the things that I adore,
All that matters and more.

INK-STAINED

I like it better this way,
Ink-stained instead of tear-stained.
I chose what I want to keep with me.
These are all beautiful things,
The things I love in life.
I'll never forget them again.

FLOWER CROWN

Use some wildflowers to make me a crown,
Set it on the top of my head and call me Queen.
I think I might feel pretty then, like someone special,
Someone important, and someone I've never been.

WILDFLOWERS

Let me stay here, let me lay here,
Let me rest in a field of wildflowers.
I am at peace in this place.
I am deep in the moment.

I haven't had this in forever.

BOUQUET

Bring me a bouquet of chamomile and lavender,
I'll breathe it in deep and fall asleep
With them held tight in my hands.

This is supposed to be healing,
This is supposed to be soothing.
This will be my remedy
From hurting terribly.

BLOOMING

I think I am blooming,
My cheeks red like rosebuds,
My face turned to the sun.

I am at my best,
Feeling my most beautiful.
I have been asleep all winter.
Now I am wide awake.

I think I am blooming,
Opening without fear,
Looking more alive.

WHO TO BE

There's something in the distance
And a faint echo of insistence—
This is where you need to go.
This is the place you need to see.
This is all you need to know:
Here you can be exactly who you want to be.

WHO I WAS

I have been mean and manipulative.
I have been selfish and self-centered.
I have been ignorant and oblivious.
I have been the kind of person
I would be ashamed to be today.

I hope I have grown since then.
I hope I have not left wounds that will never heal.
I hope I can pray and apologize for all I've done.

I was someone I was not proud of.
I was hurting to realize that.

But I have to accept my failures
In order to one day move forward.
I hope I'm taking the right steps.

WHO I AM NOW

We are built on the bones of the people who wandered into our lives. Some of them came to us through coincidence, while others entered by design. Our bodies have known air cycled through other lungs. Our minds have echoed words uttered by others. Our wounds were stitched by healers before we could learn to do it ourselves. Someone else showed us a way to walk and talk and now we have to decide to copy them, or improve upon their teachings. We are not made to be replicas, especially those who caused hurt.

I do not want to be hurt or cause hurt or know hurt. I do not want to play those games when the rules change with every player. But that is an inevitability. That is what we will have to face. It is not a game, but a reality. We are not always kind, but I hope most people try to be. Even those who are hateful and cruel, I hope they do not mean harm. I hope they recognize when they are violent with speech or touch or even a wrong sort of look. I hope they recognize that wrongness and search for ways to correct it. To change. To be kinder, softer, gentler. To be someone with more heart and more willingness to learn and grow as someone capable of love and care that all people deserve.

Who I am now must be better than who I was. And if I am not that, then I need to do more. Sometimes I may falter, or even fail, but I will dust off my bloody knees and tie back my hair. I will clean myself up, then lower myself to my knees again and apologize. Let me bow. Let me fix my mistakes. Let me lower myself before you because how I've failed and know that when I rise again, I will be better than I was before. Determined and stronger and set to earn a place in your life.

There was a battle in my mind and I was on both sides of it. I was offender and defender, I was warrior and protector. I was the sword and the shield. And now I am the builder, trying to create a new world out of the rubble. Sometimes I have to start over when I've fucked up the foundation. Sometimes I get it right when I take my time to ensure everything is in its right place.

It may be true that no one is perfect. I am afraid of my own flaws, my own defeats. I am terrified at looking back where I walked and seeing the steps I left behind, the path I carved with every decision. I hope it wasn't drawn in violence and gore, that I haven't watered my gardens with blood. I hope there are flowers growing in the grass I've trampled across. I hope that the walls I pushed aside are still standing.

Who I am now is much different than who I was before. I only hope I am better. I only know I have to keep trying to be.

ACKNOWLEDGEMENTS

I always have so many people to thank, but I'll keep it brief.

Thank you to my loved ones. Thank you to my mom for raising me to be who I am and for doing so much to learn about mental health and how to be there for me. Thank you to my sister for being there when I need you most. Thank you to Angelica and Andrea for being the best friends I could ever have. Thank you, Vanessa, for being the person who understands parts of me others cannot.

Thank you to my writing community. To the Toronto Writer Crew, especially June Hur, who feels more like a sister than a friend and who means more than I ever imagined I could find in a writer friend. To my agent sibling, Rachel Brittain, for always cheering me on. To my agents (past and present), because even though you don't represent my poetry books, your support in my writing has meant so much. To Liselle Sambury, Roselle Lim, Faridah Àbíké-Íyímídé, and Marina Hill, thank you for the enormous encouragement and believing in my writing.

And thank you to the readers of my poetry. I never really knew I'd go down this path in my writing career, but I'm grateful for the support you provide in reading this work.

About the Author

Kess Costales is a Filipino-Canadian author and poet. She currently resides in Toronto, if not lost in daydreams. Though she holds a Honours Bachelor of Science in Psychology and Criminology from the University of Toronto, story-telling has always been her fate. In chapters or verses, she has found a way to grow and heal and love life. She strongly believes in destroying the stigma around mental health, especially for people of colour, and makes it a significant part of everything she writes.

You can follow her on Twitter, Instagram, Pinterest and Wordpress (@kesscostales).

Lightning Source UK Ltd.
Milton Keynes UK
UKHW010721091020
371301UK00001B/41